OUTDOOR SCIENCE

HABITATS

Sonya Newland

www.waylandbooks.co.uk

First published in paperback in Great Britain in 2022 by Wayland

Copyright © Hodder and Stoughton Limited, 2019

 Produced for Wayland by
White-Thomson Publishing Ltd
www.wtpub.co.uk

Editor: Sonya Newland
Design: Rocket Design (East Anglia) Ltd
Illustrations: TechType
Consultant: James Thomson

ISBN: 978 1 5263 0942 6 (hbk)
ISBN: 978 1 5263 0943 3 (pbk)
10 9 8 7 6 5 4 3 2 1

Wayland
An imprint of
Hachette Children's Group
Part of Hodder & Stoughton
Carmelite House
50 Victoria Embankment
London EC4Y 0DZ

An Hachette UK Company
www.hachette.co.uk
www.hachettechildrens.co.uk

Printed in Dubai

Picture acknowledgements:
Alamy: Roger Parkes 16t; iStock: Anghi 5t; Shutterstock: Svetlana Foote cover tl, Ocskay Bence cover tr, D. Kucharski K. Kucharska cover bl, Sari Oneil cover br, Aleksander Bolbot 4tl, Christopher Robin Smith Photography 4tr, Henderbeth 4ml, Diana Mower 4mc, Anna Grigorjeva 4mr, rjmiguel 4bl, Matt Tilghman 4bc, Brian Kinney 4br, Rich Carey 5b, photka 6t, Volodymyr Burdiak 6bl, ShaunWilkinson 6bml, Stefan Pircher 6bmr, Wolfgang Zwanger 6br, Volodymyr Burdiak 7tl, Vaclav Sebek 7tr, L.A. Faille 7bl, Sharon Haegar 7br, Butterfly Hunter 8(1), Cloudpost 8(2), 21 bml, kzww 8(3), Aleksandar Grozdanovski 8(4), iiiphevgeniy 8(5), Vova Shevchuk 8(6), Carol La Rosa 9t, Wildlife World 9m, Marek Velechovsky 9b, AndreAnita 10t, Sai Kyan Mine 10bl, Sainam51 10br, Dr Morley Read 11t, saiko3p 11ml, Rudmer Zwerver 11mc, Dagmara Ksandrova 11mr, moonoi172 11bl, Edvard Mizsei 11bm, Rostislav Stefanek 11br, Yana Vasileva 12t, Peter Gudella 12m, Tatahnka 12b, Isarapic 13t, Isarapic 13b, Rostislav Stefanek 14t, Zerbor 14bl, Nataly Studio 14bml, Potapov Alexander 14bmr, rolfik 14br, optimarc 15tl, Thorsten Spoerlein 15tr, Sergey Dubrov 15ml, Sergei Brik 15mr, Designua 15b, Viktor Sergeevich 18t, Jirovo 18mt, Fotikphoto 18mb, Mizantroop 18b, Jordan feeg 18–19, Thipwan 19t, Kelp Grizzly Photography 19b, Joe Sheekey 20, yothinpi 21tl, kamnuan 21tr, de2marco 21tml, skydie 21 tmr, Henrik Larsson 21 bmr, Elena Schweitzer 21bl, SGM 21br, Jan Holm 22t, voronas 22ml, Lizard 22mc, Alex Coan 22mr, prapat1120 22bl, Opas Chotiphantawanon 22bm, Jiang Hongyan 22br, Alta Oosthuizen 23t, Heather Lucia Snow 23m, NatalieJean 23b, Ventura 24t, Cathy Withers-Clarke 26tl, Aureliy 26tr, Capricorn Studio 26b, R-Tvist 27tl, DutchScenery 27tr, Zerbor 27ml, Kostsov 27bcr, Eric Isselee 27mct, 27mr, 27bl, 27bcl, happymay 27mcb, Jiang Hongyan 27br, Rawitz 28t.

Illustrations on pages 16, 17, 24, 25, 28 and 29 by Tech Type.

All design elements from Shutterstock. Every effort has been made to clear copyright. Should there be any inadvertent omission, please apply to the publisher for rectification.

The website addresses (URLs) included in this book were valid at the time of going to press. However, it is possible that contents or addresses may have changed since the publication of this book. No responsibility for any such changes can be accepted by either the author or the publisher.

Contents

What are habitats?

Habitats are particular places where plants and animals live.

Habitats around the world

Habitats provide animals with food, water and shelter.
A habitat can be as big as a desert or as small as a leaf.

Different habitats have different features.

forest

grassland

desert

woodland

meadow

coast

rainforest

ocean

Micro-habitats

Micro-habitats are small habitats within big ones. A single tree in a wood is a micro-habitat. So is a patch of earth and grass in a meadow. A micro-habitat might have different features to the bigger habitat it exists within.

An old log is a micro–habitat. Certain plants and insects may live in and on it.

Habitats under threat

Habitats are precious places, but all over the world humans are damaging them. People cut down rainforests, throw plastic into the oceans and build houses over meadowland.

Plastic pollution is seriously damaging ocean habitats.

Changing habitats

If a habitat changes, there might not be enough food and shelter for all the animals that live there. That means they have to compete with each other for these resources. There are other problems, too. Some animals only eat certain plants. If those plants are destroyed, the animals that eat them may also die out.

HANDS On!

Rubbish that is not thrown away properly can harm the environment. Why not help your local habitats by picking up litter you see lying around? Make sure you use a litter picker or wear gloves.

What lives where?

Different types of animal need different things from their habitat.

What are habitats like?

The features of a habitat include:

* how much sunshine it gets

* the amount of space or shelter it provides

* what the soil is like

* how much water there is

* the plants that grow in it

Bigger animals usually live in larger habitats because they need more food, water and space.

Hot or cold? Wet or dry?

Some animals like cool, damp places...

Others like warm, dry places...

Others can survive in places with hardly any water.

Some need to live completely underwater...

Living together

Animals help their habitats in all sorts of ways. Worms turn over the soil, letting in air, which helps plants grow. Cockroaches eat dead plants, then put the nutrients from them back in the earth. Bats and birds spread seeds through their droppings, which creates new plants.

Amazing adaptations

Some animals have adapted special features that help them survive in their habitats.

SPOT IT!

Look around you. How is our habitat suited for humans to live in?

Elephants have big ears, which they flap to keep cool.

Polar bears have thick fur to keep them warm in the icy Arctic.

Ducks have webbed feet to help them swim in their watery habitat.

The colour and pattern on a leopard's fur help it hide in the grass.

Animal identification

Animals belong to different groups, called classes. Animals in the same class have similar features. A classification key is a list of questions that can help you identify different animals by their features.

You will need:
* a notepad
* a pencil
* a copy of the classification key below

Step 1

Copy the classification key below, then look at the pictures. Answer the questions to work out which creature goes where in the key.

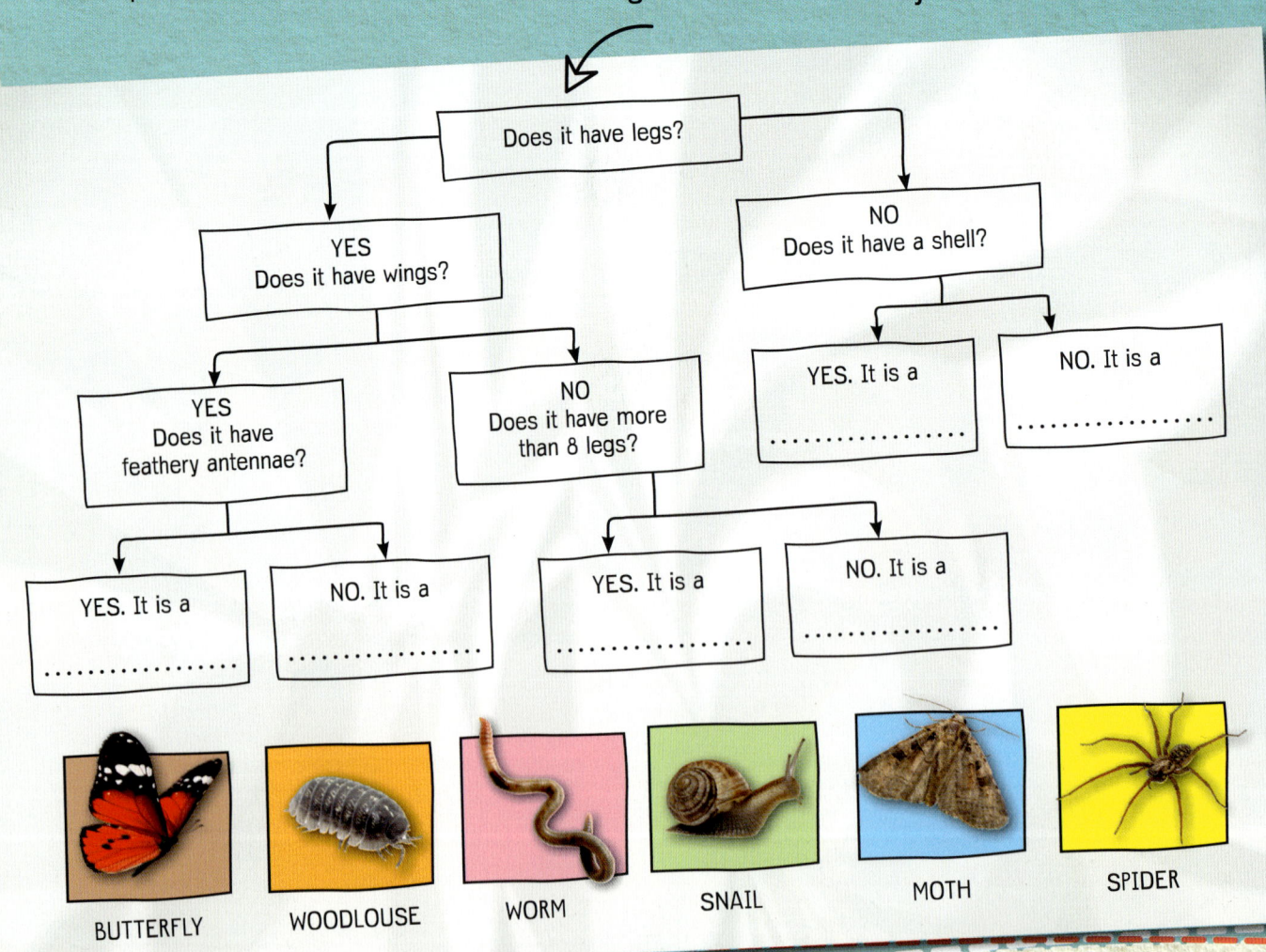

Does it have legs?

YES
Does it have wings?

NO
Does it have a shell?

YES
Does it have feathery antennae?

NO
Does it have more than 8 legs?

YES. It is a
....

NO. It is a
....

YES. It is a
....

NO. It is a
....

YES. It is a
....

NO. It is a
....

BUTTERFLY   WOODLOUSE   WORM   SNAIL   MOTH   SPIDER

Step 2

Go outside and find somewhere to sit quietly. Look at the creatures around you. Think about the features that make them similar to or different from one another. Write a list.

Step 3

Now note down some questions that you could ask that would group together animals with similar features. Here are some ideas:

Does it have a tail?

How many legs does it have?

Is it covered in fur?

Does it have feathers?

Does it have a shell?

Can it fly?

Is its body divided into several segments?

Step 4

Create your own classification key with yes or no questions to help someone identify the animals you have seen. You could draw pictures to help them decide!

WHY NOT TRY? Go to a different habitat such as a woodland or a pond and look at the animals there. Create a different classification key with yes or no questions to help someone identify the animals you have seen.

food chains

The pattern of who eats what in a habitat is called a food chain.

Producers and consumers

The plants and animals in a habitat are all connected. All these living things can be put into one of two groups – producers or consumers.

producer
Producers are living things that make their own food. Plants are producers because they create their own food using energy from the Sun.

consumer
Consumers eat other living things for food. They may eat plants or other animals.

Predators and prey

Predators are a type of consumer. They are animals that hunt other creatures for food. The animals they hunt are their prey. Many animals are both predator and prey.

...but a spider is also prey – birds, toads and lizards all make a meal of spiders.

A spider is a predator because it catches and eats flies and other insects...

Apex predators

The most fearsome consumers are apex predators. These are the animals right at the top of the food chain. They are not hunted by other animals. Not all apex predators are big. An insect called a preying mantis is an apex predator.

A preying mantis can kill and eat creatures three times its size.

Who eats what?

Sometimes plants and animals are eaten by more than one other creature in a habitat. When that happens, the pattern is known as a food web. The arrows in a food chain mean 'is eaten by'.

SPOT IT!

Can you identify any food chains or food webs in nearby habitats?

Woodland habitat food chain

fruit   mouse   owl

Pond habitat food chain

algae   tadpoles   fish

Habitat hunting

Go on a habitat hunt to find out what lives in micro-habitats nearby.

You will need:
* a piece of paper
* a pencil
* a magnifying glass

Step 1

Walk around slowly, looking for places where animals might live. Look down at the ground and above you, as well as around you. Look for piles of leaves, areas of tall grass, or in the bark of trees.

UNDER BARK

Not much light.
Damp and shady.

Some moss growing on bark.

Step 2

When you find a micro-habitat, write the name of it in your notebook. Then note down the features of the habitat. Think about sunshine, water, plants, flowers, soil, bark, leaves, etc.

Step 3

Using your magnifying glass, look for living things. Draw a tally chart and write down all the different creatures you can see. They might be insects or bigger animals. Keep a tally of how many of each creature you see.

Step 4

Now find a different micro-habitat. Write another list and chart to see what different plants and animals live there.

Step 5

When you have explored three or four different micro-habitats, compare them. What do you notice? Are the plants and animals different in each one? Have you seen the same animal in two different habitats? If so, what other similarities are there between the habitats?

✷ Do the same plants grow in both habitats?

✷ Are they both warm and dry or cool and damp?

✷ Do they get the same amount of sunshine?

SPOT IT!

Can you identify a food chain in each habitat?

⚠ REMEMBER

✷ Be careful not to disturb the animals too much when looking at habitats. Go quietly and move things like stones and rocks carefully.

What's in the pond?

Some animals need to live in and around water. A pond is the perfect habitat!

What is a pond?

A pond is a small area of still water, like a little lake. Ponds are usually quite shallow. Some ponds may be created naturally. Others are made by people to encourage pond life to their garden or local park.

Pond plants

Plants need water to survive, so ponds are the ideal environment for many plants. Some floating plants grow right in the pond itself. Their roots may be buried at the bottom, or they may just hang in the water. Other plants grow in the damp soil near ponds.

Some plants grow completely under the water.

Types of plants you might see in and around ponds include:

trees like willows

bushes like hawthorn

wildflowers like buttercups

water plants like water lilies

All kinds of animals

From birds to tiny insects to mammals, all sorts of animals use ponds.

Water birds such as ducks and swans glide on the surface.

You might also see pond skaters, water beetles or pond snails on the surface of the water.

You may be able to spot fish, leeches or mussels under the water.

At the edge of the pond, visitors might include snakes, beavers or deer.

frog

frogpawn

froglet

tadpoles

four legs

two legs

Frog life cycle

Frogs belong to a class of animals called amphibians. Amphibians are special because they can live both in and out of the water. Frogs are born in water. Baby frogs, called tadpoles, breathe through gills. Later, they develop lungs so they can breathe air and live on land.

Make a mini-pond

Create your own pond habitat!

You will need:

* an old washing-up bowl or another watertight container
* two or three small pond plants and plant containers
* gravel or small stones
* rainwater

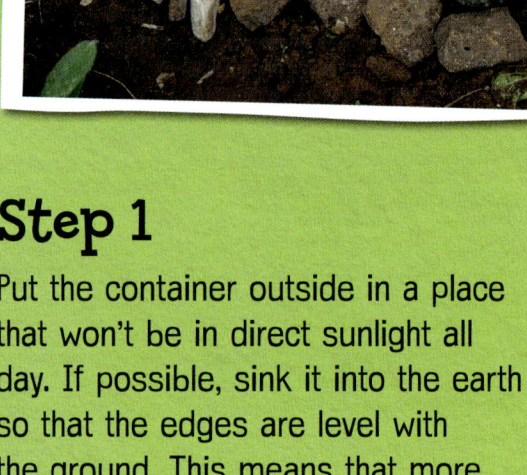

Step 1

Put the container outside in a place that won't be in direct sunlight all day. If possible, sink it into the earth so that the edges are level with the ground. This means that more animals can come and go. If you can't dig down, use bricks or logs to create 'steps' for animals to get into and out of the pond.

Step 2

When your pond is secure, put a layer of gravel or small stones on the bottom. These help keep the water clean, and create a healthy habitat.

Step 3

Fill your pond with rainwater. You can get this from a rainwater barrel if you have one. If not, just wait until it rains! Do not use water from the tap. This contains chemicals that can harm wildlife.

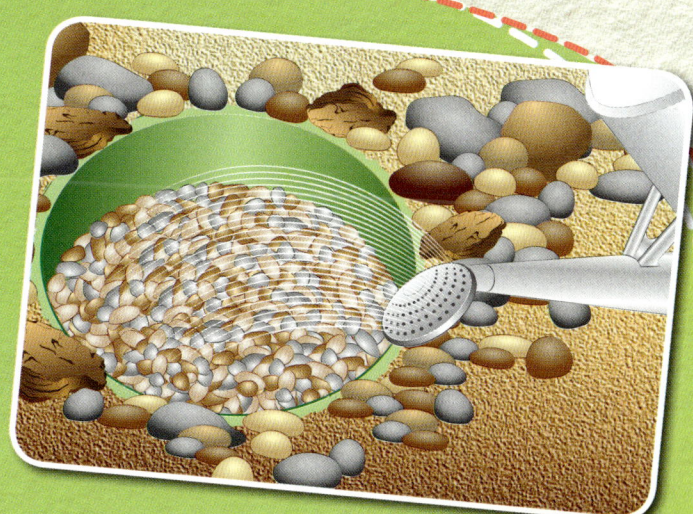

Step 4

Add your pond plants. Arrange them so that they just poke up over the surface of the water. That way they can provide shelter for animals.

Step 5

After a few days, start to watch your pond. Sit quietly near it, or watch through a window. What animals do you see in and around it?

! REMEMBER

* Sometimes slimy weed grows in ponds. To get rid of this, wind it round a stick and gently pull it out of the water.

Log life

Rotting wood may not seem like a nice place to live. But old logs are a perfect home for some small creatures.

From tree to log

A living tree is a micro-habitat for lots of creatures. When a tree falls and dies, it becomes a log. It begins to change, and then it becomes a different type of micro-habitat.

Invertebrates

Invertebrates such as insects and spiders like old logs because they are dark and cool. These creatures burrow under the loose outer layer and eat the soft, rotting wood.

Birds nest in the branches of a tree.

Squirrels eat the fruit and nuts.

Insects burrow in the tree's trunk.

Insects lay their eggs in the damp darkness behind the bark.

Birds

Birds know that logs are alive with minibeasts. The birds peck away at the log to find their favourite food.

SPOT IT!

Look up into the branches of a tree. Can you spot any bird's nests? How many?

Birds also use logs as a resting place.

Mammals

As the middle of the log rots away, it creates a space that animals can use for shelter. Foxes make dens in old logs. A hollow log also makes a good tunnel or bridge for small animals like squirrels or mice crossing the forest floor.

These marmots have made their den in an old log.

Minibeast hunt

Next time you're out and about, go on a minibeast hunt. How many insects you can identify?

You will need:

* this book
* a notepad
* a pencil
* a magnifying glass

Go to a woodland area and find a rotting log. Carefully lift it up. What creatures can you see? Use the photographs opposite to help you identify them. Make a note of how many you see.

① REMEMBER

* Get an adult to help you lift up the log and put it back again after you've been on your minibeast hunt.

centipede
* long, flat body
* segmented body
* 30 to 60 legs
* one pair of legs per body segment

millipede
* long, rounded body
* segmented body
* between 40 and 100 legs
* two pairs of legs per body segment

caterpillar
* long, rounded body
* hairs on body
* fleshy horns on head
* several pairs of legs

beetle
* three body parts
* six legs
* two pairs of wings
* antennae

woodlouse
* grey or brown body
* 14 body sections
* about 1 cm long
* can curl into a ball

slug
* grey or brown body
* short tentacles on head
* saddle-shaped patch behind head
* flat bottom to body

snail
* grey or brown body
* long tentacles on head
* shell
* flat bottom to body

spider
* two body parts
* bigger abdomen
* eight legs
* up to eight eyes

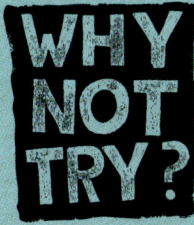

WHY NOT TRY?

When you have identified a minibeast, follow it to see where it goes. For example, follow a trail of ants backwards and forwards. What are they doing? How far can you follow your minibeast before you lose track of it?

Rock pools

Rock pools are a micro-habitat. They are found on seashores.

Sheltered shores

The seashore is the area where land meets the sea. It is a special habitat because it is home to creatures that like salty water. Features of this habitat include rocks, sand, pebbles, seaweed and pools of salty water.

Life in a rock pool

Have you ever seen a rock pool? These small pools of seawater can be found on the parts of the beach that are covered and uncovered as the tides come in and go out again.

Hundreds of different species make their home in a seashore habitat.

All sorts of living things make their home in a rock-pool micro-habitat.

starfish

limpet

goby

shrimp

crab

seaweed

A changing environment

The rock-pool environment is always changing. If it is sunny, the pool can get very warm. If it is rainy, the rain makes the water in the pool less salty. The amount of water changes with the tides and the weather. Animals in the rock-pool habitat have to be able to adapt.

Unusual animals

Anemones look like plants, but they are really animals. They have lots of tentacles. Each tentacle is covered with hooks. The anemone uses these hooks to catch its food – fish and shrimp.

Barnacles are sea creatures with a hard outer shell. They spend their whole lives attached to rocks or the bottom of boats. They even attach themselves to bigger sea creatures like turtles and whales.

Sea urchins are round, spiky sea creatures. Their mouth is on the bottom of their body, so they can easily eat their favourite food, algae.

⊘ REMEMBER

✴ When exploring the seashore habitat, make sure you know when the tide is coming in so you don't get trapped.

Name that shell!

A shell is a hard outer layer that sea creatures create to protect themselves. When the animal dies, its shell is left behind.

You will need:

* a net
* a jar
* a bucket or other plastic container
* a notebook and pencil

Step 1

Go for a walk along the beach or seashore. Pick up as many different types of shell as you can find.

Step 2

When you have a good selection of shells, lay them out on a tray so you can see them. Arrange your shells in size order, from biggest to smallest.

Step 3

Look carefully at each shell.

* Is it long or more rounded?

* Does it have a whorl (a spiral shape)?

* Is it made up of two halves?

* Is it rough or smooth?

* What pattern of grooves or colours does it have?

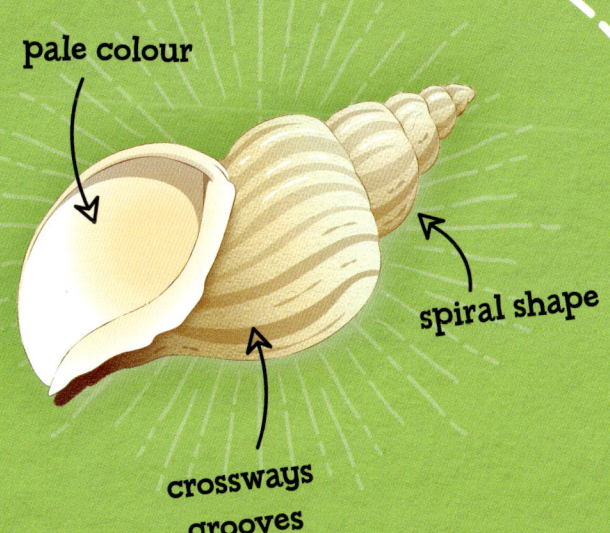

pale colour

spiral shape

crossways grooves

Step 4

Use this chart to identify which animal the shell came from. Sketch each shell and label it.

whelk

cowrie

cockle

venus clam

oyster

clam

mussel

limpet

tiger cowrie

SPOT IT!

Look inside some shells on the seashore. Can you spot anything in them?

In the grass

Fields and meadows are large, open spaces. They are usually covered in grasses and wildflowers.

Tropical grasslands are called savannahs. They are warm all year round.

Temperate grasslands, such as prairies and steppes, are warm in summer and cold in winter.

Alpine meadows are high up in mountains. They have short summers and long, cold, snowy winters.

The meadow micro-habitat

Not all meadows are huge habitats. Small fields and meadows can be found all over the world. Even a tiny patch of grass and flowers in a meadow can be a micro-habitat for hundreds of creatures.

Minibeasts in the grass

Sit in a meadow and you'll soon realise that it's crawling, jumping and buzzing with life. Spiders, ladybirds, beetles, grasshoppers, worms and caterpillars find everything they need in long grass. They can eat it, shelter in it and hide in it.

Grasshoppers are camouflaged by the grass. This hides them from birds that would eat them.

Bees and butterflies love meadows. They collect pollen from the flowers.

It's all connected

An ecosystem is all the living things in one area. The meadow ecosystem is made up of plants such as grasses and trees, and the insects that live in them. Bigger animals are also part of this ecosystem. What might you see if you look carefully?

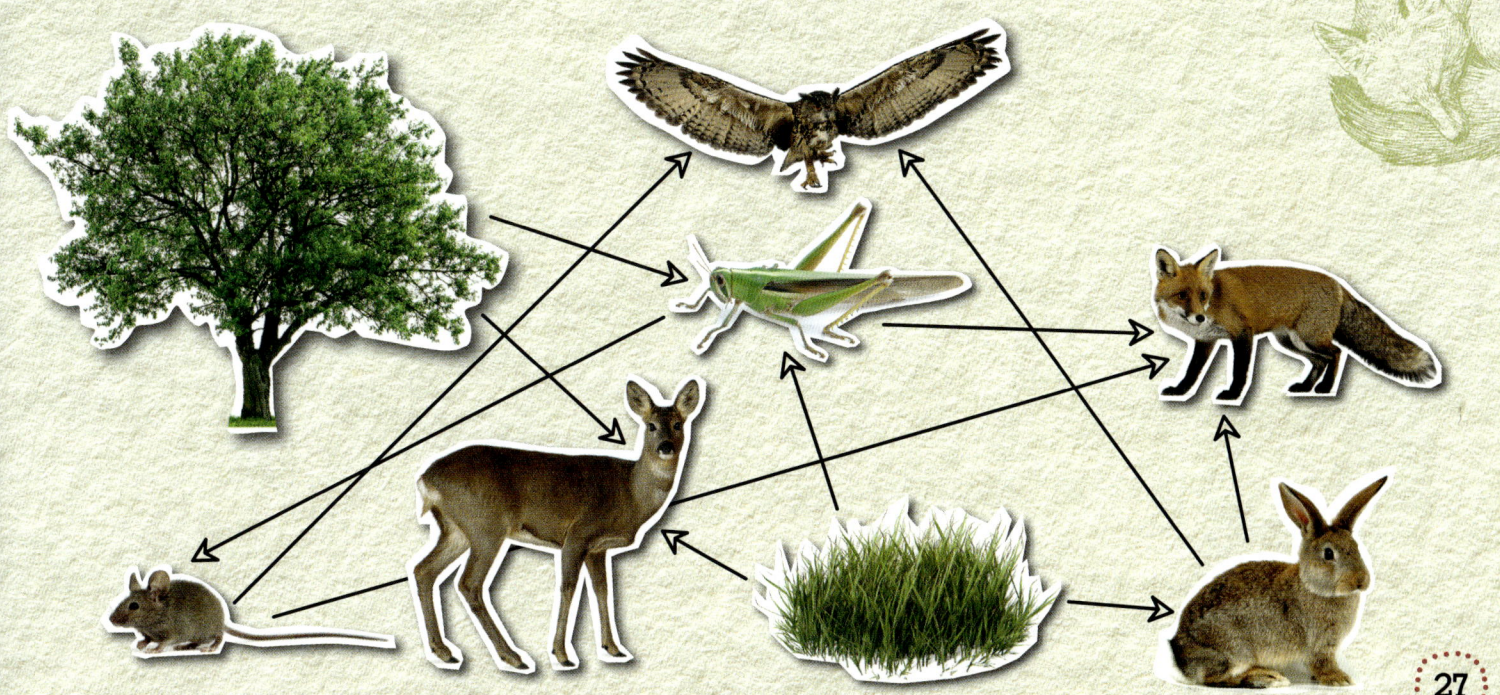

Be a habitat hero

All over the world, habitats are under threat. You can help by taking care of a micro-habitat near you.

You will need:
✳ a tape measure
✳ a notebook
✳ coloured pencils

Step 1

Choose a tree in your school grounds or near your home. You are going to make sure that this micro-habitat is kept safe for the animals, birds and insects that live there.

Step 2

Draw a picture (or take photographs) of your tree in whatever season you begin this project. Get to know how it looks. What kind of tree is it? Does it look healthy? What colour are its leaves?

Step 3

Spend some time watching the creatures that use the tree. What birds sit on its branches? Are there any nests? If so, how many? Do squirrels scamper up it? Can you see insects crawling around on and in the bark? Which ones?

Step 4

Visit your tree regularly and write down any changes you see. Do you think they are natural changes – for example, due to the changing seasons? Or are they because of outside factors, such as things that people are doing near the tree.

Step 5

Take care of the area around your tree. Keep it free of litter. Watch for anyone climbing the tree or breaking off branches. If you see this, tell an adult. Make sure your tree habitat is kept safe and healthy.

WHY NOT TRY? Make a poster about your tree. Include some things you have discovered about it. Include a message about the importance of looking after habitats.

Glossary

abdomen – the back part of an insect's body

adapted – changed in order to survive in a particular environment

algae – a type of plant that lives in water

amphibians – a group of animals that live in water and on land

camouflaged – when an animal is well hidden because the colour of its fur blends into the background

classification key – a series of questions that help you identify an animal

compete – to try and gain something by defeating another creature

ecosystem – all the plants and animals that live and work together in a particular place

gills – slits on the side of the body that allow animals to breathe underwater

invertebrate – a group of animals that have no backbone

mammals – a group of animals that have fur and give birth to live young

moss – a soft, spongy plant that often grows on dead wood

nutrients – substances that living things need to grow and survive

pollen – the dusty substance inside flowers that helps make new plants

pollution – harmful substances that damage the natural world, such as chemicals in the air or plastic in the oceans

predator – an animal that hunts other animals for food

prey – an animal that is hunted for food by another animal

resources – useful things that help humans and animals survive

tide – the movement of the sea as it goes in and out along a coast

further reading

Books

Animals (Outdoor Science)
by Sonya Newland (Wayland, 2018)

Get Outdoors: A Mindfulness Guide to Noticing Nature
by Paul Christelis and Elisa Paganelli (Franklin Watts, 2018)

Habitats (Science Skills Sorted)
by Anna Claybourne (Franklin Watts, 2017)

Websites

Explore habitats and the natural world using the BBC's wildlife webpages.
www.bbc.co.uk/nature/habitats

Find out more about habitats and other facts about nature and conservation.
http://wildlife.durrell.org/kids/fun-factsheets/habitats-factsheet/

Index